Nursing Wounds

Mark James

BookLeaf
Publishing

India | USA | UK

Presentation by *BookLeaf Publishing*

Web: www.bookleafpub.com

E-mail: info@bookleafpub.com

ISBN: 9789363304796

First edition 2024

To Dean, River, and Zoey I love you more than anything.

ACKNOWLEDGEMENT

Baby Bird, we both know I wouldn't have made it very far at all with out you.

PREFACE

There is still no such thing as bad art, so here is some more of mine.

waking nightmare

Each and every day when I get up I go oh fuck
Because no matter what I have to get up
Telling you why would be whining at worst and
pandering at best
but I'm sure you know the feeling

There's never any rest
Everyone must have you, though you're fare
from the best
others wallow, bed rotting is a thing
albeit i think its very fringe

but for me, and probably you, there is so damn
much to do
and if we don't no one else will
and worse even when we do, no one seems to
notice
your going through the motions because you
can't just lay down

others can and do, and as much as I desperately
don't want to, I get up
So much hurts, but I do the things to go do the
things

other people don't, they simply don't, and they
get away with it
but I don't get that luxury

Moonlit Sonata

In the wee hours of the morning, someone
expired, seemingly unnoticed and alone.
Everyone knew that we had a deceased patient,
and for reasons of beauracracy and decency, we
had to let them rest in the room they had passed
in.
Somehow the moonlight didn't make the patient
look pale, it made their skin look warm, as if the
warmth of the sun had been reflected into the
deceased from thousands of miles away.
As a student I had the luxury to sit and keep
company with the dead, as it was offensive for
them to be alone at the end.
We shared our life story without exchanging
words, learned everything there was to know
about the secrets of the universe without
divulging them.
Hours dragged on, I tended my living patients,
and would round on my most terminal patient as
if they could still benefit. After the sun came up
they were finally moved to more permanent
resting arrangements.

Interlude

Success is only success when it feels like success, ask any successful person and they will tell you they don't feel successful. Ask any happy person and they will say that they feel successful. When I acheived so much objectively I didn't feel successful, and aside from being mentally enriched, I have very little to show for my pursuit of success. In reality the success I experieenced was an excess of anxiety, and emotional deterioration to the point of utter and complete vexation causing a nervous deviation to alienation from all my reason and desire to acheive success. These days I seek rest and comfort and the only time i feel joy is when my children are around and laugh and play and i get to experience a little moment of success

Nuts and bolts

5

Understand this, you understand nothing.
Break through in flight, wing warping,
then explain the bumble bee or helicopter,
what knowledge you have is improper,
the closer to knowing the deeper the faith said
the scholar
so no matter your rise and rate
accept the truth of the human fate
whatever we try, from your mind to wring
the whole of it amounts to nothing

tell me about my parents

you want me to share fond recollections of your
parents, when I barely know my own
anxiously I fumble for a story with a start a
middle and an end that will bring you comfort
and warmth
What I find are almost glimpses of concepts that
I was too young to grasp when I knew them.
If only they had recognized and drawn out my
independent mind things could have been so
different
Across the chasm between us, I now think we
might have been kindred spirits
Smoke messages sent of passive acceptance and
kindness
Never judgemental, never rude, never harsh
In fact they are probably the only adults I have
met that left no scars.
Nowhere was I when you needed an epitaph,
for years I was unaware they had died
I offer up this which doen't make amends by half
through my memories i have scried
Your parents were a kind refuge in a world of
malice and though to you and my anxiety that
thought does not suffice, the reality is that that

made them giants the likes of which we may not
find again

Relaxation

hot water washes over me in waves of sound
drums crash with a force to match the beat of my
heart, and the syncopating rhythm slows my
anxious racing
guitars growl and whine like wrestling dogs
brought to order
voices growl and chant sentiments from my
subconscious, sometimes more coherent than my
best articulation, and other times with all the
clarity of an ancient bog in front of me, the
musicians pace the stage like caged tigers, or
bob their head like apes or birds of prey
behind me the crowd surges and spins,
seemingly as dangerous as a riptide, but
ultimately safer than a lovers embrace.

HR

Always lock your computer when you walk
away, whether for a moment, but especially at
the end of the day.
Your friend that landed you this job, has been
rather strange of late, would love to come across
your email, a la watergate
Surely your colleagues are professional, they
will simply lock it up and not mind at all
Except they won't, they'll they'll dig for non
existent dirt and try to turn on you for caring
more about the patients
What could I do when the two of you frog
marched my patient away before theyy had
received their due
Nurses on the floor were more than annoyed,
that with our patient's well being your colleagues
had toyed
Checking boxes, but not knowing why, it was
time to punch the clock and go by the by
You wanted to give them the best care, sir that
simply will not do.
An email had been sent, explaining the situation,
with hopes of sincere exhoneration, but the
others had a different explanation.

How dare I break ranks with them, never mind
what a problem they had been
No harm no foul, even with a life at stake, that is
how we like to win
I care about the patient and what, if we don't do
our job, could be
That doesn't matter, you are dead to me
A wolf in sheeps clothing, trying to lure me into
a trap, because i did not worship them, I must
shut my yap
Refusing made things hard, but not impossible,
and caring for my patients to the degree they
deserved was my just reward
After enough time and horror, the problems were
resolved and i heard I'm sorry, but never having
to second guess the safety of my patients was the
big reward

Against Death

I am not against death, I am against indignity
the indignity of dying too young, the indignity of
not getting to say goodbye

Tough enough

As a new nurse I was eager to prove myself, I fell into the trap of thinking that showing up on time, with a smile, and doing my job to the best of my abilities was surely the righteous path to success and happiness.

In short order I discovered that my wants, thoughts, needs, abilities, knowledge, and skills would always take a back seat to the needs of others, I was cast out from the safe predictible order of preop, and sent to the post anesthesia care unit.

Fortunately for me all of my patient's were ASA3 or better and everyone got a block and a block. It was learning to PACU from nurses that were anything but, with training wheels, and I had a chipper disposition in those days.

Certainly I was in the more critical area with more critical patients because I was so smart and on the ball.

No no, not that.

You are with the grumpy and mean nurses and
you are there because you don't cry after being
around them.

This is so much better for you.

Just go do the job, you'll figure it out.

what really matters is that you don't cry about
the other nurses.

Patient care first.

No that angers your colleagues.

Fuck.

Depression

There is a weight on me that I cannot shake.

Constant is this burden which holds me down,
holds me back

Worried people think its all fake

Voices whisper of course it is, you're a hack

It is mine to carry and though my moods and
experience does vary I find the will to tarry

here

in this moment

where for a few seconds my burden is lighter
because I can see the wonderous beauty

What rapture

the sun rise

this flower

a sign in the window of a house that says you
matter

a random statue

and for just that second when the universe
speaks and the burden eases

even then I cannot lie

I am still weighted by the immeasurable burden

but life is still wonderful

Here it is

There is an entire subculture around mental
health, and the lack there of,
and I still can't find help.
Everything is acceptable and okay, and no one
understands what is going on with me.
Here it is, my mask, that I carefully constructed
onsheer instinct.
It protects against everyone, and I barely notice
it
except when the person who is supposed to be
helping me simply shrugs and goes you know
what to do
Oh you're so smart, this isn't really going to help
you
but its right here, I'm telling you, stop looking at
the mask
I'm obviously hiding behind my intellect
its called intellectualization, where I can justify
all the awful shit and be okay with it
its one of the foundational layers of my mask
Shouldn't you be explaining this to me?
Why can't you see my mask, here it is, right out
in front
wait a minute,
you want to see the mask, it is so well contrived,
Why isn't anyone trying to see me?

Circulator

I see what's happening here,
non provider greatness, for you its strange
You think you're the boss, it's adorable, and it's
nice to see that doctors never change
So open your gloves lets begin, yes it's really
me, your nurse, take it in
I know it's a lot, the cap the scrubs, when you're
staring at a nursing god
What can I say except you're welcome, for the
bed and the trays and the lines
Hey it's okay, it's okay you're welcome, I'm just
an ordinary nursey guy
Hey! What has two thumbs and keeps us on
time, when you're talking nonsense? This guy
When the rooms too cold who got you warm
stuff in your bowl? You're looking at him yo
Oh also I lassoed Ad-min (you're welcome) to
stretch your block and have some fun
Also I turned on suction, to keep your field clear
and such
What can I say except you're welcome, for the
trays i got in SPD
Hey it's okay, okay you're welcome, I guess its
just my way of nursing
you're welcome, you're welcome

Well, now that I think of it
Doc I could go on and on, I can explain every
common going on, the trays, the grafts, the
chart, that was just me messing around
I talked to a vendor, ordered up lunch, here it
comes now, lots of hummus
So what is the lesson, what is the take away,
don't mess with nurses when we're on a smooth
day,
Well anyway let me say you're welcome, for
this awesome O R flow
Hey it's okayit's okay you're welcome, well
come to think of it I've got to go
Hey it's okay to say you're welcome, I need you
to vac that smoke
I'm walking away, away, your welcome, cuz this
nurse can do anything but overtime
You're welcome,
and thank you!

Lovely Bouquet

Perfectly arrayed wild flowers
Blanket the spring desert in sublime beauty
yet this divine precision is only a paltry attempt
to create a bouquet worthy of you
so immense are my love and adoration that even
nature guided by provenance cannot create
beauty worthy enough to be gifted to you

Release

Throttle pinned, speedometer maxed, everything
falls away
Howling, screaming at the top of my lungs,
vision fades at the edges
the anguish screwing them shut against gushing
tears, as my eyes match my throat spewing pain
Cars around me seem still as I streak past, all is
still behind wet glass
Something uncoils from my heart, screams
subside into wracking silent sobs, my howling
abates
the world around speeds up as I ease off the
throttle, the engines roars subsiding to a calmer
growl
acceptance
this is actually happening
I may actually be dead
Certainly I am leaving the life I built, to go into
the unknown facing possible death, and though I
did it once before it is entirely a different thing.
Stillness within
Acceptance?
Peace
Death
the end of the life I had known

a premonition of the wickedness to be visited
upon me
hours later no tearful goodbye from my lover,
our children gotbig happy hugs before we left
the house
now I shoulder this burden without so much as a
kiss goodbye
One of us is hoping I am dead, I am mourning
the life I am leaving,
but I accept this death, and it doesn't bother me
that its what she wants
hollowed out
numb
that last ride is a happy focal point
as an empty vessel on an empty plane
heading towards the largest empty city

Summer

Smog closes in again, shielding me from the
beauty of the world
A fitting raiment for my despair,
isolated by pain and toxic air,
my heart and lungs screaming
Summer is a joyous time for others,
for me it is a time of breaking over and over
As I saved others, but cannot save myself

Rosey glass

Grieving a life that never was, I long for the life
I wanted to live

every day my heart breaks for how much i miss
my children and experiences that never were

in the warmth of the noon day sun I shiver and
there is no hope for tommorow or aa better way

Nostalgia suffocates while the witch who is
architect of my demise prods me with burning
irons

agonized and despairing I stumble along with
compassion and grace, trying to lift the burdens
of others while crushed by my own

goodness and kindness cost nothing and cannot
be wasted, but surely they are wasted on the
monster who bore my children

like a bad comedy sketch she runs the wrong
direction fighting imagined threats and fearing
demons that never were

an appalling balance where i long for the
Heaven we never had, she flees a hell that never
was

silently screaming the children suffer as i sue for
peace while my world burns again and again

no respite comes, and when i imagine something
has gone right or will be okay, another snare
takes my feet from under me

another hook drags me around, my goals and
hopes spinning crazily away from my
beseeching hand

everyone looks on in sympathy, no one offers
help, and the whirling dervish dances on

Melinda

Warm brown eyes looking into my own,
promising warm love forever

skin so very soft, lips brush my heart and soul,
two hearts become one

arid desert plain, paradise in a person, loving
anticipation

hearts beat in sync, ecstatic collapse, truly and
deeply

Manifesto1

Pompous bloated corpses
dictate what we do
vehemently they deny
any truth we prove
flaunting power undeserved in the light of day
after years of servitude, ignore them,
it's time to make them pay
society is flaking
its a stale croissant, so it's time
let the guillotine drop

Hustle

No time to bleed, and while I look away time
takes what I need.
A thousand minor hurts compound while I'm too
busy to heal, what was ignored is now beyond
repeal.
Limping across the finish line, there's not
enjoyment or celebration,
Apartheid this victory of mine.

Manifesto 2

Lacking fidelity the self appointed elite fear the faithful, lashing out with jeweled pompous pumps.
Lacking comprehension, what is right and wrong, they fear any contradiction of their thoughts.
Weakness drives despotic and ineffectual control.
All it would take to fix the system is for those who think they're better, swallowing their vitriol.

Yukon

More than a few women have been on the back
of my motorcycle, not a boast, just a fact
　　How I behaved with that one should have
tipped me off to how blatantly I was in denial
Every single one of the other's: friends, first
timers, one nighters, proracers, long term lovers
I protected
　　My entire being focused on keeping them
wholly defended, safe and secure
Frighteningly different, everything I did with
this one was wrong
　　Showboating, not focused, my behavior
wholly disparate compared to normal
Never obvious, self harm rarely looks like it, this
instance no different
　　Part of the self watches foolish laughter,
taking downright noxious action
Looking back at someone not loved
　　but someone that lavished adoration, a
reprieve from the realities in which
　　there was only drowning
Intoxicated by pretense, swallowing lies, flying
through the night in a way that should have
caused fear
Exhausted from fighting alone for one year

This lie felt good
		Convinced of invincibility
Woke in a hospital, next day discharge to
purgatory, not hell, as seemingly there was
recovery from leaning into the untruth,
	though it cost the little headway fought for
and won
	before the accident
Where I met Annie, and almost could not see
through her, no articles, just vague rumors from
well wishers, my own mind well and truly
scrambled
Thankfully there was no hobbling, and it never
came to murder, all it killed was my bike, self
respect, sanity, and reputation